Earthsteps

A Rock's Journey through Time

Diane Nelson Spickert

Illustrated by **Marianne D. Wallace**

FULCRUM
GOLDEN, COLORADO

Earth was formed about 4,600 million years ago.

First surface water, algae forms, oxygen in air

Precambrian

Carboniferous

Seed Fern

Devonian

Silurian

Ordovician

Cambrian

Insects

Fishes

Nautiloids

Antiarchs

Trilobites

360 million years ago

410 million years ago

435 million years ago

500 million years ago

543 million years ago

Geologic Timescale

The geologic timescale is based on more than 200 years of scientific work. A timescale helps place rocks, fossils, and geologic events in their correct historical time sequence based on both relative and absolute time. Worldwide fossil assemblages or groups of fossils from sedimentary rocks were used to name the relative time periods, such as the Jurassic and Cretaceous. Radiometric age-dating methods were used to determine absolute time, the millions of years spanned by each time period. To determine a rock's approximate age in millions of years, scientists measure the products of unstable radioactive elements, called isotopes. Our story begins 250 million years ago during the Permian Period and progresses to present day.

Geologic Timescale

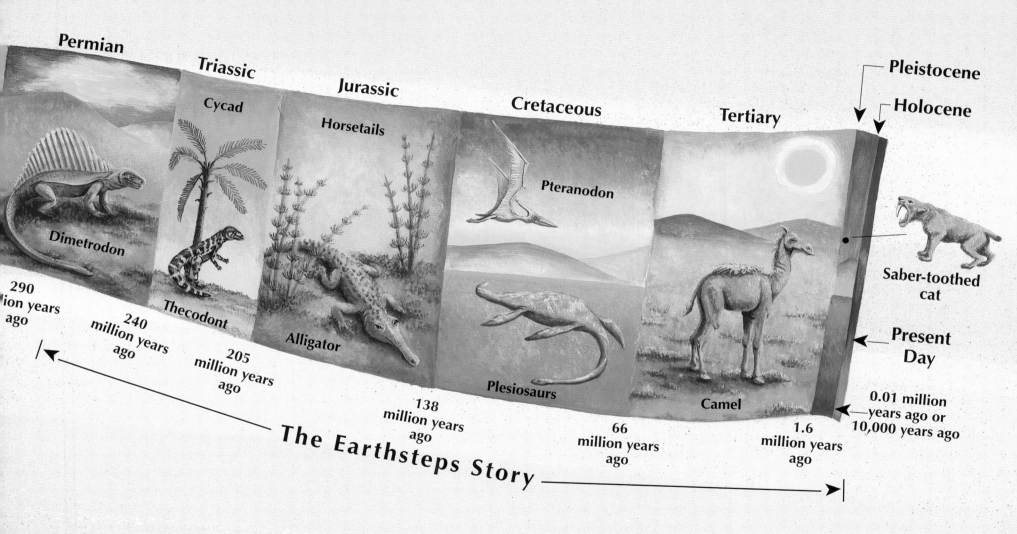

Permian

Triassic

Jurassic

Cretaceous

Tertiary

Pleistocene

Holocene

Cycad

Horsetails

Pteranodon

Dimetrodon

Thecodont

Alligator

Plesiosaurs

Camel

Saber-toothed cat

Present Day

290 million years ago

240 million years ago

205 million years ago

138 million years ago

66 million years ago

1.6 million years ago

0.01 million years ago or 10,000 years ago

The Earthsteps Story

The cold wind danced over a mountaintop one spring night 250 million years ago. Water froze and expanded in a jagged crack, wedging loose a square, speckled rock. The rock hurtled down the cliff and landed with a muddy spray on a rock pile. *Thwap!*

So began the journey.

Moonlight bathed the black-and-white-speckled rock. The rock's **mica** crystals twinkled at the starry sky. Imbedded in the **alluvial fan**, the rock overlooked a shallow pond. On both sides rose the valley's **granite** walls.

Permian conifers surrounded the pond. Massive trees raised powerful cone-laden branches toward the morning sunlight. The air filled with fragrance and roared with the buzzing and clicking of a thousand insects. Shimmering green beetles burrowed into a rotting log.

Summer after summer, windblown sand blasted and polished the square rock, which balanced precariously as raindrops **eroded** the surrounding mud. *Crack!* The ledge broke, and an **avalanche** swept the rock into the pond. Several pieces chipped off when it landed on a rock pile and rolled to a stop four feet below the water's surface.

Through the years,
the pond grew into a lake.
Rocks formed a natural **dam**
until the water rose and a stream broke through.
The current rolled the rock violently end over end
across the lake and down the mountainside.

The rock sat at the bottom of the new stream. The water flowed slowly. Smaller rocks bounced past, but the square, speckled rock was too big. Slimy green **algae** grew on its edges, and hungry fish swam by and pecked. Huge ferns grew along the stream's banks, and the air was heavy with moisture.

Each fall, thunderstorms filled the stream. Finally, rushing water lifted and carried the rock. Even **boulders** bounced in the strong, cold currents. As it rolled with the other rocks in the stream, the speckled rock became smaller, rounder, and smoother. Small pieces chipped off along its path and left a sparkly trail.

Each year, fall ended when winter arrived with a soft, white cover of snow. The rock nestled in its frozen hiding place. Wind blew layers of blue ice. Fish hid in the deepest water.

Twenty-five million years passed. The speckled rock, smooth and polished, inched down the mountain in **Triassic** time. Towering conifers and palmlike **cycads** filled the landscape. The land was sunny year-round, and reptiles scoured the earth, devouring insects.

At the bottom of the mountain, the stream joined a swiftly moving river. The water crashed like thunder. Narrow, sandy beaches lined the banks.

The rock rolled along the river bottom like a marble and dug a straight, deep line in the sand, pointing out the direction of flow. Sticks carried by the water dragged along the bottom and left marks too.

An ancient **thecodont** reptile drank along the riverbank, its scaly green skin glistening in the sunlight. It stepped on the rock, pressing it into the brown, slippery mud. The thecodont sniffed the air, then scampered off in search of prey.

Other rocks rolled and bounced past the
speckled rock, which was stuck in the mud.
But after several weeks, the mud washed away
and the rock broke free.

Seventy-five million years went by. Rivers came and went. They moved sideways across the earth, shifting course. The rock was carried by a new river, wide, warm, and murky brown. It meandered through hot, humid horsetail swamps. **Jurassic** alligators lounged on big crescent-shaped beaches that filled the bends. They eased quietly into the water, then lunged at passing fish.

Finally the river came to the salty ocean. The tiny rock was spit onto the delta, where the river dumped its **sediment** load. Rocks, sand, mud, and tree branches landed in a pile at the river's mouth.

There lay the rock. Huddled in the muck, segmented sea worms burrowed around it. Clams hid snugly beside it. Beyond the **delta**, in the endless blue ocean, a striped blue-green **plesiosaur** swam. Millions of silvery fish darted quickly away as the huge beast twisted its long, glistening neck to catch one. Paddlelike fins propelled the large reptile into dark water to continue the chase.

Years passed and the rock didn't move. Then one evening, gloomy black clouds darkened the sky, rain beat down, and wind whipped the coastline. With a gigantic *whoosh* the mud bank gave way and the rock was swirled into a sandy, salty stew.

A wave swept over a nearby beach and dumped the rock into a jumbled pile of sand, shells, and seaweed. Now too small to be a rock, the pebble lay, a sparkle at the bottom of the heap.

Over the next 50 million years, ocean waves pounded the beach continuously. The pebble was uncovered and dried in the hot sun. Large, toothy **Cretaceous** seabirds searched for fish. They sailed gracefully, inches above the water's surface, dipping and snapping. Sprinkled along the coastline, the earth's first flowers blossomed in muted colors.

Pulled by the tide, the pebble sank into deep water. Then the waves threw it back onto the beach. Forward and back, forward and back, the pebble rolled in constant motion until finally it was ground down to a grain of sand.

This ended when a more
powerful storm hit. Uprooted
palm trees flew through the
air like dandelion seeds.
Gigantic waves ate huge
bites out of the beach.
The ocean swallowed
the sand.

Swept far out to sea through an underwater **channel**, the grain of sand was quickly buried in a thick layer with other grains. The large grains dropped to the bottom; the small, lightweight grains landed on top. They rolled, jostled, and settled—cracks, dents, and nicks lodged together into a comfortable position.

Year after year, layers of sand rained down. The shimmering grain was buried thousands of feet below the ocean's surface, and the layers became thicker and deeper. The sand grain could not move.

Over the next 30 million years, the Cretaceous ocean above the sand grain filled with sediment and the salt water dried up.

Thousands of feet above the speckled grain, *Triceratops* walked heavily, bellowed its warning to *Tyrannosaurus*, and lowered its horns for battle. The world was changing, and soon the dinosaurs would be gone.

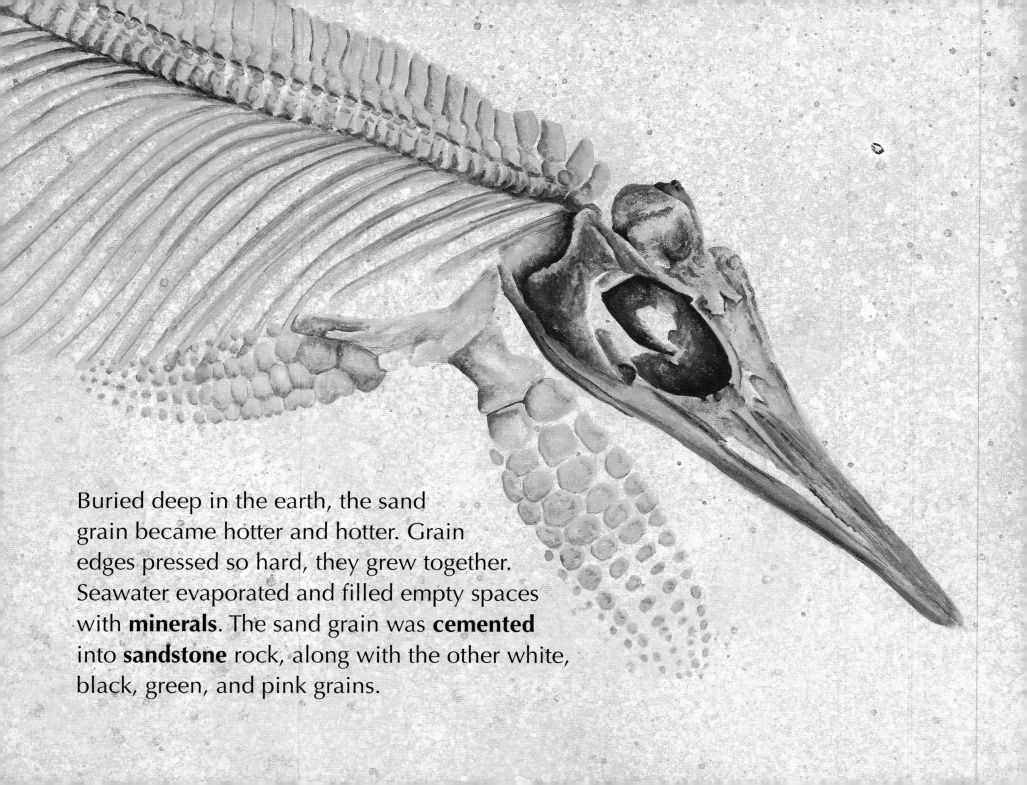

Buried deep in the earth, the sand
grain became hotter and hotter. Grain
edges pressed so hard, they grew together.
Seawater evaporated and filled empty spaces
with **minerals**. The sand grain was **cemented**
into **sandstone** rock, along with the other white,
black, green, and pink grains.

A few million years passed, and the sandstone started to cool. **Fault** cracks broke through the earth, and big blocks of rock pushed slowly skyward. Where the ocean used to be, mountains rose. Once again on a mountainside, the sand grain twinkled in the blazing sun, tearing wind, pelting rain, and freezing snow and ice.

A million years before now, in **Pleistocene** time, **saber-toothed cats** with long, ripping fangs roamed the land and roared their ancient songs at the moon.

Tonight the cold wind dances over a mountaintop. Water freezes and expands in a jagged crack, wedging loose a square chunk of sandstone carrying a speckled, sparkly grain. The rock hurtles down the cliff and lands with a slushy spray on a rock pile. *Thwap!*

So begins the journey.

Glossary

Algae: Simple plants that live in water.

Alluvial fan: Mass of sediment deposited by a stream or river where a mountain meets a plain.

Avalanche: A rock or snowslide falling down a mountain or over a cliff.

Boulders: Large rocks over ten inches across.

Cemented: Grains bound together by mineral cement in a sedimentary rock.

Channel: A long, low depression carved by moving water, such as a river.

Conifers: A group of plants dating back to the Permian, about 280 million years ago. Modern pine trees belong to this group.

Cretaceous: A period of geologic time ranging from 66 to 138 million years ago.

Cycads: A group of plants dating back to the Late Triassic, about 200 million years ago, some of which resembled modern palm trees. A few cycads live today.

Dam: A barrier that keeps water from flowing.

Delta: Mud and sand that builds up where a river reaches the ocean and loses energy.

Eroded: To wear away the land surface.

Fault: A break in the rocks where the earth has moved.

Granite: A coarse-grained igneous rock made up of mostly quartz, feldspar, and mica minerals. An igneous rock cools from a hot, molten liquid called magma.

Jurassic: A period of geologic time ranging from 138 to 205 million years ago.

Mica: A mineral that splits into thin sheets.

Mineral: A naturally occurring solid substance with a crystal structure and consistent chemical composition.

Permian: A period of geologic time ranging from 240 to 290 million years ago.

Pleistocene: A period of geologic time beginning 1.6 million years ago and ending 10,000 years ago.

Plesiosaur: A marine reptile that lived during Jurassic and Cretaceous time.

Saber-toothed cats: Large, extinct cats with two long, sharp canine teeth that lived during the Pleistocene Epoch.

Sandstone: A sedimentary rock with sand-sized rock particles held together by a mineral cement.

Sediment: Rocks, sand, silt, and clay worn and broken off from other rocks.

Thecodont: A large reptile from the Triassic Period that walked on two legs; an ancestor of true dinosaurs.

Triassic: A period of geologic time ranging from 205 to 240 million years ago.

Triceratops: A three-horned vegetarian dinosaur that lived in the Late Cretaceous Period.

Tyrannosaurus: A meat-eating dinosaur that walked on two legs and lived during the Cretaceous Period.

Bibliography

Agashe, S. N. *Paleobotany: Plants of the Past, Their Evolution, Paleo-environment and Application in Exploration of Fossil Fuels.* Enfield, NJ: Science Publishers, 1997.

American Geological Institute. *Dictionary of Geological Terms.* Rev. ed. New York: Anchor Press/Doubleday, 1976.

Beerbower, J. R. *Search for the Past: An Introduction to Paleontology.* 2nd ed. Englewood Cliffs, NJ: Prentice-Hall, 1968.

Boardman, R. S., A. H. Cheetham, and A. J. Rowell, eds. *Fossil Invertebrates.* Cambridge, MA: Blackwell Science, 1987.

Case, G. R. *A Pictorial Guide to Fossils.* New York: Van Nostrand Reinhold, 1982.

Dott, Jr., R. H., and D. R. Prothero. *Evolution of the Earth.* 5th ed. New York: McGraw-Hill, 1994.

Fenton, C. L., and M. A. Fenton. *The Fossil Book: A Record of Prehistoric Life.* New York: Doubleday, 1989.

Hansen, W. R., ed. *Suggestions to Authors of the Reports of the U.S.G.S.* 7th ed. Reston, VA: U.S. Geological Survey, 1991.

Lambert, D. *The Field Guide to Prehistoric Life.* New York: Facts on File Publications, 1985.

Moore, R. C., C. G. Lalicker, and A. G. Fischer. *Invertebrate Fossils.* New York: McGraw-Hill, 1952.

Parker, S. *The Practical Paleontologist.* New York: Simon & Schuster, 1990.

Shimer, H. W., and R. R. Shrock. *Index Fossils of North America.* 10th ed. Cambridge, MA: M.I.T. Press, 1977.

Steel, R., and A. P. Harvey, eds. *The Encyclopedia of Prehistoric Life.* New York: McGraw-Hill, 1979.

Sutcliffe, A. J. *On the Track of Ice Age Mammals.* Cambridge, MA: Harvard University Press, 1985.

Van Eysinga, F. W. B. *Geologic Time Table.* 3rd ed. Amsterdam: Elsevier Scientific Publishing, 1978.

Whitten, D. G. A., *The Penguin Dictionary of Geology.* With J. R. V. Brooks. Middlesex, England: Penguin Books, 1972.

To my husband, Charlie, for his support, and to my sons, Cameron and Andrew, for their inspiration.

—Diane

To my sons, Zeb and Ben, who first introduced me to the prehistoric world.

—Marianne

Printed in China
0 9 8 7 6 5 4 3 2 1

Fulcrum Publishing
4690 Table Mountain Drive, Suite 100
Golden, Colorado 80403
800-992-2908 • 303-277-1623
www.fulcrumbooks.com

Library of Congress Cataloging-in-Publication Data
Spickert, Diane Nelson.
    Earthsteps : a rock's journey through time / Diane Nelson Spickert ; illustrated by Marianne D. Wallace.
        p. cm.
Includes bibliographical references.
Summary: Describes the geological setting for the transformation of a rock to a grain of sand over the course of millions of years.
    ISBN 978-1-55591-730-2 (pbk.)
    ISBN 978-1-55591-986-3 (hc.)
    1. Weathering—Juvenile literature. [1. Weathering. 2. Historical geology.] I. Title: Earth steps. II. Wallace, Marianne D., ill. III. Title.
QE570 .S65 2000
551.3—dc21   00-009196